not
by
sight

not
by
sight

true stories from an amazing journey

DEBBY GREEN

XULON PRESS

Xulon Press
2301 Lucien Way #415
Maitland, FL 32751
407.339.4217
www.xulonpress.com

Paperback ISBN-13: 978-1-66287-998-2
Hard Cover ISBN-13: 978-1-66287-999-9
Ebook ISBN-13: 978-1-66288-000-1

Dedication

To Stephanie,
I am so very grateful
For all you are and do;
My life is so much richer,
So, Sweetheart, this one's for you!

CONTENTS

INTRODUCTION

Decades ago, in another life, I was in the process of losing my sight. My uncle Elrose Zook encouraged me to tell my story. I did that in the book *Debby* by Deborah Zook. So much has happened since then. I've lost most of my sight and have learned to navigate life as a blind person. My relationship with God has deepened though, and I understand that we do not walk relying on what we see around us. Rather, as we draw closer and closer to Him, we learn to "walk by faith, not by sight" (II Cor. 5:7). This short book started out as a collection of poetry, but there were stories and they needed to be told, so now you have both the poems and the stories of just how we walk by faith throughout our lives, yours and mine. My prayer is that you will be able to relate to these stories and they will help you grow closer to God as you journey through your life.

PROLOGUE
IT'S A BEAUTIFUL DAY

What an absolutely beautiful day,
A time for peace and rest;
To spend time with the love of my life,
To know I am favored and blessed.

Sometimes I get pretty busy
I need time to just be still;
To hear the birds and feel the breeze,
A time to seek His will.

So I'm spending time in God's presence,
His love flows through each vein,
The candle's lit, the coffee's hot
And I'm listening to the rain!

chapter one
THE WATER SLIDE

One summer day, my daughter Stephanie and her two sons, Carson and Dane, ages seven and ten, were visiting. There was a new water park in town and it seemed like a fun place to visit. It was a warm sunny day and so off we went. Stephanie found a place where we could put our things and she could keep an eye on us. I slid into the pool, splashing around in shoulder deep water. I did not know where the boys were but before long, ten-year-old Carson called to me from the edge of the pool.

"Want to go down the slide, Gigi?"

Of course I did. I had not known there was a slide and it sounded like fun.

"Are you going down with me?" I asked. That was important to me.

"Yes, I'll go with you." He answered.

One more question, "Have you been down it yet?"

"No, not yet."

I followed the side of the pool until I reached the ladder and climbed out. Carson was waiting for me. I picked up my cane with my right hand and he took my left hand. Off we went. We soon reached a flight of metal stairs.

"Here are the stairs." He explained. I felt the first step with my cane and with Carson ahead of me, we climbed a flight of stairs, probably thirteen or fourteen steps. I could tell with my cane when we had reached a landing.

"So, is this where the slide is?" It seemed like a logical question.

"No, there is another flight of stairs."

I was surprised but, no problem. He guided me around a corner and there it was, another flight of stairs. And up we went. As we reached the landing, I realized that we were now two stories up. This would be a great slide.

"So where is the slide?" I asked.

He hesitated only a moment and then said, "It's not here. We have to go up one more level. Are you okay with that?"

We had come too far to go back now.

And then we were on the next landing.

"Is this where the slide is?" I was almost afraid to ask.

Then someone asked, "Are you going down the slide?" It was an adult, probably a park employee.

"Yes, can you show me where to go?" Carson was standing behind me. "Are you coming down after me?"

"Yes," was his tentative response. Perhaps he was having second thoughts. I learned later that we had climbed forty-five steps and were roughly thirty-five feet up at this point, like standing on the roof of a three-story building. Looking down from that platform was probably a lot scarier for Carson than it was for me at that moment.

The adult guided me to the top of the slide. I reached down to see where I would start and sat down at the top of the slide. But I had one more really important question.

"So there is no way I can get hurt going down this slide, is there? It is safe, right?"

"Oh, yes, totally safe. One of our people is waiting at the bottom. Ready?"

I pushed off wondering if he had ever been down this slide blindfolded. But there wasn't time to ponder that thought too long. In a few seconds I hit the first sharp curve and banked to the left. Then there was a dip, a bump, and a sharp turn to the right and then I lost track. I was trying to anticipate what might be coming next when all of a sudden, with no warning, the slide ended. I splashed into the water and sank straight to the bottom!

The water in the catch trough was not over my head, and I got to my feet quickly. Some guy was saying something about getting out of the way of the next person. He guided me to the side of the pool where there was a ladder. I was climbing out just as Carson hit the water behind me. "Are you okay, Gigi?" He asked as he climbed out behind me. He was concerned.

I was laughing, "Yes, I was great. It was fun!"

In reflecting on that experience, I at first thought that I perhaps should have asked more questions. Perhaps I should have known that the slide was three stories up with lots of curves and bumps. But, maybe not. If I had known all that, I might have opted out. And just think of all the fun I would have missed.

Life is like that. We sometimes think we need to know what is coming down the road ahead of us, but maybe not. Walking by faith and not by sight changes everything. Maybe it is enough to know that we can trust the One guiding us.

The Question, Why

There are many things in life that are hard to understand.
Things don't always happen the way that we have planned.

Some storms look far too scary, Some valleys far too deep.

Some nights feel far too dark, some paths seem far too steep.

God promised not to leave us though; He said to never fear.
We may not know where He will lead, but we know He's always near.

So I'll stop asking questions; hold tight to His strong hand.
And though it makes no sense right now, I know He has a plan.

I see His warm and loving smile, His outstretched arms to me.
I hear His invitation, "Come, you can trust in Me."

And on that smile and those strong arms, I know I can rely;
My faith draws me to His embrace and past the question, "Why?"

chapter two

STEPHANIE

By my late thirties, I had been married, given birth to my wonderful little girl, Stephanie, and gotten divorced. I was a single mom working full-time and I was blind. I had moved to a different town in the mix, so I was also in a new community and a new church. Looking back, my life then looks so overwhelming but, amazingly, at the time it all seemed to work out—one day at a time—relying on God and with a little help from my friends! Yes, looking back, I was walking by faith, not by sight.

My mother was living in Pennsylvania but when she realized my situation, she was at my doorstep in a heartbeat. She lived with Stephanie and me for those early years, and she helped me in so many ways. At our first opportunity, we found a good daycare for Stephanie and when it was time, I put her in a Christian preschool where she continued through elementary and middle school.

My time with Stephanie was my top priority, though. In the early years, I childproofed the house since I could not keep an eye on her. I attached a little jingle bell to one of her shoe laces so I could hear where she was at any point in time. I found books that contained both print and Braille so I was able to read to her. We liked to play pretend. We acted out some of the stories and movies we had seen together. One of our favorites was *The Wizard of Oz*. She would be Dorothy and I would cycle through all the other characters. Sometimes, we'd played school or Hide-and-Seek. She remembers playing library where we would line up all the available books and she would be the librarian and I would check out the books. We played store where she was the "checkout lady" and I was the customer. We put puzzles together.

Her safety was essential and Stephanie understood that not holding my hand when we went for walks was not an option. We flew to visit my sister in Florida a couple of times, and especially going through the airport, Stephanie knew she must hold my hand. I did have a child leash, the kind that attaches around each of our wrists, but she hated it and I did not have to use it much. I simply had to have it slung over my shoulder, in plain view, to let her know I was serious about this holding-hands business.

I am not sure when or how Stephanie came to understand about my blindness. When she wanted to show me something, I would hold out my hand and say, "Let me touch it, Sweetheart. Mommy needs to feel it to see it." That was never a problem and she became accustomed to simply handing me things. Of course, if she was showing me something that needed my assessment, I always told her it was very pretty and that she had done a good job. One day she wanted me to see the picture she had just finished coloring. She laid it on my lap and then, taking my pointer finger, she slowly ran it over the page saying, "See, Mommy. Didn't I do a good job?"

"Yes, you did a great job." But I was confused. I asked, "Why did you do that with my finger, Honey?"

Her answer made perfect sense. "I wanted you to see it." Since I had told her I needed to touch things to see them, apparently, she reasoned, there was some sort of seeing mechanism in my fingers.

Very early on, we found a good church and began to build relationships. My new friends were amazing and offered to help in many ways. We attended all the services and got involved in every way we could. I helped teach Sunday School and soon was asked to be part of the worship team, playing the piano. Stephanie joined the Bible quiz team and we traveled with the team to other churches around the state for matches. I was able to get the 576 questions and answers in Braille, so

I helped coach, practicing with the quizzers. There was nothing really very visual about helping quizzers memorize answers to questions and learning to hit that buzzer quickly.

My favorite Junior Bible Quiz question, you ask?

Number 40: How did God test Abraham's faith when He asked him to leave Ur of the Chaldees?

Answer: By asking Abraham to follow Him without telling Him where He would lead Him. (Hebrews 11:8)

Essentially, God was asking Abraham to walk by faith, not by sight.

One day, Stephanie asked me a really interesting question. Here it is. I turned it into a little poem.

My Favorite Age

What is your favorite age of mine, my little girl asked one day.
I looked into her big blue eyes and thought what I would say.

I loved when you were tiny and I could hold you in my arms.
And when you were a toddler, you thrilled me with your charms.

When you went to school, I loved to help you learn.
To answer those many questions as your thoughts would churn.

Those days of nails and curling irons, and all those calls from boys,
Were just as good or better as I shared your hurts and joys.

The challenge of these teenage years, deciding what to do,
As you learn to know just who you are and what God
has planned for you.

I love you in so many ways, it's really hard to say.
I think the age I like the best is the age you are TODAY!

Stephanie grew up and the time came when I realized she would be heading off to college. Of course I wanted that for her, but still, it was a bit scary. As I was processing this change, I realized just how attentive and protective she had been toward me over the years. I recalled an incident at church when she was a toddler. A nursery worker had taken her to the restroom. I had been there a few minutes before and had accidentally left my cane propped up in the corner. She saw it there, and knowing that I needed it, insisted that she take it to me. The nursery team would not allow her to do that, not wanting to disrupt the service and Stephanie broke out in tears. I tried hard not to rely on her too much, but children of parents with a disability automatically take on a heightened sense of responsibility.

Once, at a church conference, I attended a breakout session dealing with single parenting. Two young ladies, not related to each other, both expressed concern about their single mothers who had disabilities. Both indicated that their mothers were so dependent on them that they did not think they would ever be able to leave home, go to college, or establish their own lives. I determined that day that this would not be Stephanie's story.

About a year away from her leaving for college, it began to hit me: things were going to be quite different for me. I found myself being sad and sometimes in tears; of course, she noticed.

"Mom, I need you to be strong for me. You have always been strong for me over the years, so please do not stop now. I guess you are just processing this early. Maybe God is doing this for me. He knows that I need to be sure you will be good before I leave." She reflected.

And then she added, "Actually, Mom, if I ever call home and realize that you are a basket case, I will not be able to stay at college."

That did it. I determined that I would be strong for her and support her in this phase of her life, too.

One day it occurred to me that her sense of responsibility for me might feel like a ministry area, an assignment from God. I thought it would be good to ask her about this. I did, not knowing what to expect.

I was right.

"Yes," she said. "I think God wanted me to watch out for you, making sure you were safe and doing what I could to help."

And so, it was time for me to let her go.

"Well," I started, "You have done a fabulous job! Thanks so much. I really appreciate all you have done. And now, I believe God is saying that He is releasing you from this responsibility. You are free to go to college and pursue His plan for you. He will send others to help me when I need help."

She understood. We embraced amid tears of uncertainty, joy, and love. And that is just what she did, both of us walking by faith into this new phase of our lives.

During the pandemic, we were not able to see each other as much as we had in the past. We actually missed being together on Mother's Day. We, of course, connected by phone which is good but not the same. So I had to write a poem for her.

Mother's Day 2020

So many things are different, more changes than we've ever seen.
Sunday will be Mother's Day and we're deep in COVID 19.

I know I won't be with you; you are too many miles away.

And even though you're not near me, there are some things I want to say.

You need to know I'm so proud of you; you're such an amazing mom . . .
And wife and professor and department chair, and I know there's more to come.

God has a wonderful plan for you; He'll guide you each step of the way.
He loves you more than you'll ever know and He's with you every day.

And there's one more thing you need to hear although this thought's not new,
You're in my heart and in my prayers And I'll always be here for you!

The years have passed so quickly but our relationship has only grown stronger. I have come to understand the difference between that mother/daughter relationship and the adult friend to friend relationship. We parents sometimes seem to think that we have the right to insert ourselves and our great wisdom into the lives of our grown children, whether they want it or not.

So, yes, Stephanie and I talk. I like to think of it as processing. It goes both ways and we value this time, often over breakfast at Cracker Barrel. She might be telling me about something going on in her life. It could be related to her spiritual journey, things with the kids or an issue at work. I love hearing her explain all this to me. Of course, I am tempted to insert myself and my wonderful wisdom into that conversation but I have learned to just listen. Until I hear . . .

"So what do you think, Mom?" or "Mom, what would you do?"

That is my cue and I then do share any thoughts I might have, silently praying for His wisdom.

Just last week as my grandson was reading that little poem about my favorite age, now framed and in Stephanie's library, and I told her, at age thirty-eight, "And if you would ask me that question today, Sweetheart, the answer would be the same!"

chapter three
SPEAKING OF MOTHERS

S peaking of mothers, we all have one. They come in all sizes and shapes and temperaments. Some are nearly saints; others are hurtful and destructive. Mine was special in a lot of ways. She was born to a poor couple in 1918. Her father was first generation from Switzerland and had trouble finding jobs. He felt that the best thing to do for his two young children was to find a safe home for them. He did, an orphanage run by a church. His plan was to come back and get them when he was able to provide for them. He did not expect it to be long.

And that is what he did, but when he came for them, they were not there. A foster family had taken them and given them a home. The orphanage people would not tell him where they were, and he was devastated. I understand he spent the rest of his life trying to connect with them. My uncle told me that from time to time, he would see a man, dressed in European style clothing, watching them from a distance. He thought that it was probably his father but they were never able to reconnect.

The foster home housed several children. The children were fed and clothed. They attended church and school. The rule there, though, was that, at the age of fourteen, the children were expected to get out and get a job and begin supporting themselves. And that is what my mother Mary did.

She found a job at a little country store in their small town. She stayed with the family who lived over the store. She worked in the store, watched the children, and did whatever tasks they needed her to do. And that is where she met my father, Leroy. He would come into the store for various things and liked the girl who was running the cash register. He was the son of a deacon in a local conservative church so his interest in this foster kid was suspect. He had a call on his life to be a pastor and that was fine with her. They got married and planted a small church in a rural community about twenty miles away. It was not long until children came along, five of us. I was the middle one.

Around the age of eight, it was discovered that I was blind in one eye. There had been no pain or any indication of a problem. My parents were diligent and found me the best medical attention possible. I ended up in a hospital in Philadelphia about four hours away. My parents had responsibilities at home so could not stay with me but every other day. Like clockwork, they would make the trip to the hospital, coming to see me. I was in the children's ward and not permitted to go into the hall, but on those days I would position myself in the doorway where I could see down the hall to the elevator. Somehow, they managed to be the last ones on so they would be the first ones off. All the rules went out the window when I saw them step off the elevator. I would make a bee line down the hall to greet them. I was totally unaware of all the sacrificing that was happening at home for me. My older brother and sister had to stay home from school to care for the younger children on those days. They took turns so that neither would get too far behind in their schoolwork. After seven weeks, the doctors were not able to discover the cause of the problem and they were now attempting to save the vision in my good eye.

Shortly after this, my parents left the ministry. We moved to Ohio for Dad to find employment, but two years later he developed a brain tumor and passed away. We children ranged in age from nineteen to five. My oldest brother was a freshman in college. He quit school and came home and got a job. He worked at a factory, supporting the family during Daddy's illness and through his death. And there was Mom, now a widow with five children. I am not sure how she did it. I am confident that her relationship with God carried her. I remember her kneeling at my bedside each night, praying for me as I am sure she did for each of us children.

By the time my father passed away, I was age twelve and functioning pretty well. I had no sight in one eye but the other one was close to normal. My vision gradually got worse though and by the time I was in college, it had decreased to the point that I needed to get some help. And that is when I saw my mother's determination kick in.

"I can't do this," I explained after a frustrating first semester of my freshman year of college. "I can't see well enough to read my textbooks. I can't see the board. I can't keep on going to college." I had been using a magnifier to read my textbooks and sitting in the front of the class to see the board. Even then, I struggled. I knew she would understand and let me drop out. I was wrong.

"Quitting is not an option, Sweetheart," she said kindly but firmly. Your brothers and sisters will be able to find jobs at a lot of places but you will not be able to. You have to get a college education." And then she added. "I will help you in every way that I can. I will go to class *with you* and take notes. I will read your textbooks to you and help you get through. Just know, you cannot quit!"

So we got in touch with an agency for the blind and they stepped in. Mom was true to her word. She never attended classes with me or read my books to me but she made sure that I had all the resources I needed. She even learned Braille and over the years would write little notes to me using a slate and stylus, no small feat!

My siblings also remember Mom's support growing up. One great memory from my older sister, Brenda, was when she was in Junior High. She had an assignment to collect samples of wood from a variety of trees and mount them on a display board. She said that Mom found an individual familiar with trees. She and Mom spent time with this person tramping around in the local forest, searching for and identifying various trees for samples. They mounted them on a display board labelling them. She recalls keeping that project for years into her adulthood.

One of my brothers, Paul Galen, is a musician who played drums in the band in high school. He recalls that when his older sister started taking piano lessons, Mom thought it would be nice if he took lessons also. He was in middle school and took lessons for a while. At some point, though, he said he told Mom that piano was not for him and asked her could he quit. "Yes," Mom said. "You can quit if you choose another instrument." "Then, I would like to play the guitar." He answered.

With no guitar and limited funds, it took Mom some time to earn and save up the money, but it happened. Mom found a good guitar teacher and my brother is still playing guitar to this day.

My younger sister, MaDonna, had a passion for children. She went to college with a major in elementary education. She recalls sharing a writing assignment with Mom. It was a children's book. She recalls Mom's encouraging words. "I think she thought I should pursue my dream of being a children's literature author. Maybe I should. Perhaps It might not be too late."

Looking back, probably the hardest thing my mother did was let me go to Kentucky for a job. By that time I was blind with only light perception. I had graduated from college and attended a rehab facility for the blind. I did have a job but did not have all the other details worked out. I would be staying with some friends for a while but then would be looking for an apartment. I am confident she had me covered with prayer. She was only a phone call away and we stayed in close touch over the years. And, of course, when Stephanie arrived Mom was there in a heartbeat, driving alone from Pennsylvania to Kentucky to be with me. And she was there for me during those early years. Mom passed away in 1990 when Stephanie was seven. They did a lot of fun things together. Stephanie got her love for reading from Mom. Her most vivid memory is seeing Mom standing at the top of the flight of stairs leading up to her apartment on one of our visits to Pennsylvania. She remembers that huge smile and commented, "I always knew that she really loved me."

Mom did not have a high school education but she did get a GED later in life. She always wanted to go to college and dreamed of being a school teacher. During the last several years of her life, she experienced that dream being fulfilled. She received literacy training and began teaching English. Some of the students were individuals who simply needed to learn to read. Others were those needing to read English as a second language.

She suffered a heart attack in her late sixties while she was with me in Kentucky. She stabilized and then returned to Pennsylvania. During the summer of 1990, each of us five kids separately made a trip to visit her, which was not planned. Little did we know that these visits with our Mom would be the last for each of us. Stephanie and I flew up for a week in August. Enjoying our time together with her, we noticed that she was slowing down although she tried hard to not let it show. One month later, we returned to Mt. Union to attend her funeral. She was ready and I am confident she was overjoyed to see Jesus and then, our father. She will be waiting for us there. I had thought that it would perhaps have been good if we had known that the visit in August would be the last time we had with her. But maybe not. Knowing that would have cast a shadow over our time together. Sometimes not knowing the future, but walking by faith and not by sight is much better. Mom saw her mission in life as raising us five children, loving us, and teaching us about God. She wrote a poem that captures her thoughts about this mission.

Five Rose Buds
by Mary A. Zook

God gave me five rosebuds and said, "They're for you
To love and to care for as I've taught you to."

They came straight from heaven; they were angels on high.
And the Spirit He gave them shall never more die.

They were tiny and fragile, so precious and sweet;
From the crown of their heads to the soles of their feet.

It was easy to love them and care for them, too.
But so many more things I wanted to do.

Their petals came open, their fragrance came out.
Their love and their beauty was scattered about.

Not only at home but wherever they went,
God's Spirit of love was everywhere sent.

You see, God is watching and sees from above.
They'll be full blooming roses, sharing God's perfect love.

I'm so glad I'm their mother and I'm sharing a part
Of the heavenly sunshine God put in each heart.

chapter four
I TRIED TO RETIRE

I worked for the state of Kentucky for all my professional career. At first, I was hired at the vocational school at Hazard, Kentucky, to teach Braille. Braille, you say? At a vocational school?

Yes, and here is the story. Again, you will see God's hand using my blindness as I walked by faith, not by sight!

The summer before, as part of a requirement for my degree at Juniata College, Huntingdon, Pennsylvania, I was required to participate in an internship for the summer. After some research, again, with Mom working behind the scenes, I applied for a summer practicum with Eastern Mennonite College in Harrisonburg, Virginia. We were each assigned a location in Appalachia for the summer. I can only imagine the challenge felt by the coordinators of the project, trying to find a spot for a blind person. But they were champs. I was assigned to a health department in the heart of the mountains in Leslie County, Kentucky. My task was to teach Braille. Even in 1970, blind people had limited opportunities in the public school system. I was given a classroom and a driver. We did some networking with other agencies, got names and addresses, and started making home visits, inviting blind individuals to come and learn to read. It was a fun summer with a surprising level of response. It seemed like a one and done event but it turned out to be the springboard to the next assignment from God.

I returned to college to complete my final semester. During that spring, I attended a rehabilitation center for the blind near Pittsburg. While there, I received a letter from the director of the vocational school in Hazard, the next county over. He was offering me a job, part-time at first, to come and teach Braille. He was apologetic when he explained that I would only have one student. He would provide a driver, and I could make connections to find others.

And just who was that one student?

Her name was Lennie. She had lost her sight at an early age and had never had the opportunity to attend school. She was now in her fifties but had never stopped dreaming of learning to read Braille. Somehow, she had heard of a blind lady who had been in Leslie County the summer before. She contacted the director of the vocational school, pleading with him to try to track that lady down and see if she would come and teach her Braille. What were the chances? But he did it and explained all this in subsequent conversations. I was anxious to meet Lennie. She was a delight. I would never have a student more eager to learn. And she did. I even taught her to write Braille using a slate and stylus.

Yes, we did locate several other students who came to the class and then were able to transition to other programs at the school.

In an effort to expand community awareness, I organized an open house at the school for people to come and get familiar with some of the tricks and tools of the blindness world. I received news coverage which attracted the attention of the agency for the blind. They worked with me and before long, I was offered a job as counselor at the new office they were opening in Hazard. Again, I saw God's hand at work. And that was my career, first as a counselor in Hazard, then a supervisor for the eastern quarter of the state and then as a counselor in a new office in Elizabethtown. I enjoyed each of these positions and while there were blindness related challenges, for the most part, my being blind was an asset for my clients.

I had the opportunity to walk alongside many individuals as they learned to navigate life without sight. I remember sitting across the desk from a new client. She was devastated. She had always wanted to go to college but instead had gotten married and had children. She decided that after the children were in school, she would pursue that dream. And now, here she was, ready to go to college but her vision was decreasing and she needed help. She was tearful as she explained that she would now not be able to go to college.

I was puzzled. I thought perhaps I had missed something.

"So exactly why do you think you cannot go to college? Do you have some other disability? Is there something you have not told me?"

She was a bit annoyed as she explained once again, "I am having trouble seeing. I think I am going blind."

I got it. I leaned back in my chair deciding where I should start. "If your vision is the only thing you are concerned about, we got this. I have gone to college as a blind person and I can walk you through that. I can help you get books in audio. I can tell you what to say to your professors. I can get you help to orient you to campus. We can do this!"

I am not sure she was totally convinced, but at least I had given her a ray of hope.

told her what the next step would be and she took it. Like me in earlier years, she could not see the end of this road, just the next step. But she took it and the next one and the next one. She received the adjustment training and special equipment she needed, attended college, and got a good job.

Years later, I ran into her at a local store.

"Are you Debby, the one who was the counselor with the blind agency?"

"Yes," I responded, not knowing who she was. I asked her to identify herself and I remembered her.

She turned to her husband. I heard her say, "Honey, this is the lady I told you about. Debby, this is my husband."

Then she turned back to me. "I will always remember the first day I came to you and told you my eye problem. I told you I wanted to go to college. I remembered how you yelled at me and told me to stop feeling sorry for myself, that I most certainly could go to college, and that you would help me."

"Yelled," I was shocked. "I do not think I yelled at you. I would never do that."

"Oh, yes you did." She was laughing now as she added. "And I needed it. Thanks."

After twenty-seven years with the state and with my daughter in high school, I had an opportunity to take an early retirement being offered by the state. What a decision? I was the sole bread winner and I could not get this wrong. I had a serious conversation with God. "Please let me know if this is what I should do and exactly when. I do not know how You can possibly make it perfectly clear to me about this, but that is exactly what I am asking."

I scheduled an appointment with the retirement office in Frankfort to go over the options. They gave me great guidance and over the next couple of weeks, through a series of events, I knew, beyond the shadow of a doubt, that it was time. I was so confident that I realized that not retiring at that time would be disobedience.

It was nice being at home. Stephanie did not have to get herself off to school nor did she come home to an empty house. And then she was off to college. I was volunteering at the church and staying busy, but I was only in my fifties. I began to wonder: did God have something more for me? Again, I asked God for guidance. Counseling was in my bones but how could I get back into that field. I did some checking and learned that if I pursued mental health counseling, I would have to go back to graduate school. That would cost a lot of money and where would I go? Still, this seemed to be the direction God was leading me in. By now, I knew about this one-step-at-a-time principle so I took that first step. I called the rehab agency where I had worked for so many years and started asking questions.

Yes, I could apply for services. Yes, they would likely be able to pay for my education and yes, Western Kentucky University, Bowling Green was offering graduate school classes in Elizabethtown. I could hardly believe it. I took the required courses over the next couple of years.

Then it was time to apply for my license as a Licensed Professional Clinical Counselor (LPCC). I had read the requirements carefully, I thought. I had taken all the required courses and I had worked as a counselor with the rehab agency for all those years, meeting the 4000 hours of supervised experience required. I sent in my application, carefully documenting my education and work experience. So when I received a phone call from Frankfort in response to that application, I was puzzled.

"You cannot count your work experience with the agency for the blind," the man carefully and kindly explained. I was speechless.

"Why not,"

"You have to be supervised by an LPCC. Was that the situation?"

I was pretty sure that was not the case. I told him I would check and get back with him. I did, and I was right. I had great supervisors but they were not LPCCs.

"So, I am starting at 0?"

"Yes," he seemed sincerely sorry. He continued." Actually, you really need to submit a different application and, if you get on our website, I can walk you through it right now."

"Well, that is a problem," I answered. "I cannot do that. You can tell me what to do and I can get some assistance with that later."

He did not quit. "Why do you need assistance to do that?"

"Well, I am blind and have trouble navigating most websites."

There was a long silence. I was holding my breath. I was thinking that this might be when I learn that I cannot do this at all. Finally, he spoke. "Blind? Why have you not told us this before now?"

"I did not think it mattered. Does it?"

"No it does not. We encourage people with disabilities to get involved in this field. But if we had known, we could have helped you more." I thought I would cry.

And he did help me. We filed all the right forms, jumped through all the hoops, and I set out on accruing those 4000 hours. This meant that I needed to find someone willing to supervise an internship, but where should I start? Someone told me they had seen a sign for a counseling office nearby. I called. No, they did not do that. Then I heard about a counselor at a church so I called him. The response was a little better. He understood and wished he could help but he did not think he had a large enough client load to make it work for me. He did have a suggestion, though. He gave me the name of another established practice. I called her and she was interested. She was willing to talk with me but she had a question. With whom did I have my liability insurance? I did not have liability insurance. She was firm when she said, "Well, you cannot walk into this office unless you have insurance. Here's where I have mine." She gave me that information. Then she added. "Call me when you get insured." So, I got some liability insurance and I called her back. She was pleased and scheduled an appointment for me to come in to talk about doing my internship. I had not yet mentioned to her that I was blind. She did not know until I rounded the counter in her reception area to follow her to her office. I wish I could have seen her face. She did not miss a beat. Using the sound of her voice, I followed her and found a seat. She was a champ. We worked out the details and I began to accrue those 4000 hours.

Later, after all the details had been worked out, I asked God just how I had missed that little detail, those 4000 hours under the supervision of an LPCC. Wouldn't it have been better if I had known about that from the beginning? He had the answer. "If you had known that you would be starting at 0 to accrue 4000 hours, would you have attempted to go down this road?"

We both knew the answer. Sometimes it is best that we do not know too far ahead. We just need to know the next step, take that step, and walk by faith! And those closed doors? They, too, are blessings, ways that God guides us.

Over the next couple of years, I got those hours; not long after that, I believed that God was guiding me to set up a practice at my church. I saw a lawyer to set up an LLC and got business cards. I began to offer Christian counseling to the people at the church as well as the community!

chapter five
NEVER ALONE,
MY SENIOR PARTNER

I n the Bible, we read many names for God, many roles for Jesus, and many characteristics of the Holy Spirit. God is our Father and defender and friend. Jesus is our Healer, our Savior, and Lord. The Holy Spirit is our counselor, our guide, and comforter. It seems that whatever we need, our triune God can meet that need. In 2012, Pastor Jeff Schexneider preached a sermon series on the Holy Spirit. He identified several roles of the Spirit as outlined in scripture. One of those was a "Senior Partner." That clicked with me.

For a number of years leading up to this, I had been in the habit of doing a spiritual annual review. It could take several forms. Sometimes it was an afternoon off on my birthday where I would check out from my usual responsibilities and spend time alone with Him. Sometimes it would happen around New Years. It sometimes would turn into a retreat. One of my favorites was simply checking into a hotel across town on a Thursday evening and checking out on Saturday morning. I would be armed with a Bible, a journal, a good book, and food. Sometimes, I would be at a place that served breakfast, which I would take advantage of. Other times, I would do a partial fast. I just would not leave the hotel. God and I would have quality time. I would read my Bible and talk with Him.

The Junior Bible Quiz question that applies here is "What is prayer?"

The seemingly obvious answer is, "prayer is talking to God."
I can still hear the Quiz Master's response, "That IS incorrect for A minus five points. The correct answer is, prayer is talking WITH God." Big difference.

So at these retreats, I talked with God. My talking was not usually on my knees interceding. It was more pacing around the room baring my soul; often it would be in the form of journal entries, pages and pages, on my laptop. One time, I recall writing for hours. I had lost track of time. I had said everything I wanted to say, prayed for everyone I could think of. I was emptied out. In the pause that followed, I felt He asked gently, "Is that everything? Anything else you would like to say?"

Yes, I was done, but then something occurred to me.

"Do You have something You would like to say to me?" I asked.

I think He was smiling when He answered, "Actually, I do."

I realized that while He absolutely wanted to hear me out, what He would say to me was far more significant than anything I might want to say to Him. And I listened. That went in my journal as well. Sometimes I would imagine that He would say, "I need to see you in my office."

As I would walk into that imaginary office, I would notice a folder open on His desk in front of Him. I knew it was my folder.

"Have a seat and let's talk. Is that alright?

I would imagine that He was flipping through papers, looking over His notes.

"Let's start with the good things that happened this past year." And He would help me think about the things that I did well: successes I had in ministry and in my personal life. He was pleased and I was happy.

And then He would say, "There are some areas where you could do better. Can we talk about those?"

And we would. I would take notes and set goals and walk away armed to do better and more determined than ever to please Him.

Perhaps this is why the Senior Partner role from that sermon clicked with me.

We are in this together.

Once, I felt the need to point out the obvious to Him. "So we are in this partnership. You are my Senior Partner. That makes me the Junior Partner. Right?"

"Yes, that's right." We were on the same page so far.

"I just need You to know that I am under no illusion that in this 'partnership' You bring far more to the table than I do." That was the understatement of the century.

"Yes, you are right," He agreed. "But there is something that you need to remember. What you bring is important. I cannot accomplish my mission on earth without you and the millions of others like you. Your role is essential, don't forget that."

Over the years, I have found other ways to connect with Him. In my journaling, I often write as though I am talking to Him, and that seems to be a good way for me to express myself. When I am finished discussing the particular issue, I like to imagine what He would say in response if He were sitting across the room. Then I start a new paragraph, put in an opening quotation mark, and write what I think He would say to me. At first, I was at a loss as to what He would say. How could I possibly know that? But, actually, we do know Him from His Word, from sermons, from anointed songs, and from trusted friends. We have the promise of His guidance. So yes, we do have a pretty good idea of what He would say.

It is refreshing to go back and read through these conversations from time to time.

On other occasions, I have imagined that I've heard a knock at the front door. When I go to the door, I see that it is Jesus. I am surprised but happy to see Him. I, of course, open the door and invite Him in. "No," He would say. "I do not want to come in. I was just checking to see if you wanted to go for a walk."

Of course I did. "Sure, let me get my shoes on."

"Okay, I will just wait here on the porch."

And He would sit down and wait as I hurried to get my shoes.

Within a minute or two, I would step out onto the porch and we would start up the street. "So, is there a reason why You wanted to go for a walk with me today?" I was curious. Actually, there is. We need to talk about something."

And we would.

So, here is the question. If that really happened, what do I think He would want to talk with me about. And just what would I need to process with Him. Often on my actual walks, that is exactly what I am doing, processing things with Him.

Over the years, I have continued to grow in this relationship. I think this is His desire for each of us. As is the case with any relationship, this takes time and effort on our part. It can include praying, listening to sermons, reading good books, or spending time in nature. It certainly must include time spent in His Word. The more we read what He has written, the more we will understand how He thinks; then we will begin to think like He does.

Who's Talking

What a blessed experience
To be on our knees in prayer;
We pour out our hearts to our Father,
He understands each care.

He says to pray without ceasing;
He collects each tear we cry;
He is our Abba Father
And He understands each sigh.

But when we're done interceding
And we're ready to get on with our day,

We need to pause for a moment,
He might have something to say.

Because if we are in God's presence
Whether a short time or long
And we are the only one talking,
Something is really wrong.

chapter six
RUNNING BLIND, 1000 MILES

S omewhere in my early sixties, I heard about a lady from North
Carolina who, at the age of eighty-plus, was running a marathon.
That started me thinking. I realized that running was something I had
always wanted to do. Of course, being blind, I had ruled running out
long ago. But at that moment, thinking about the obstacles she had
overcome, I began to think that it might be possible for me to run. Of
course, I would need to find someone who could be my guide but per-
haps the bigger issue was getting into shape.

I figured I had nothing to lose so I bought myself a treadmill for
Christmas that year. I found one that was perfect for me. It had thumb
controls for both the speed as well as the incline. The buttons on the
control panel were slightly raised so I could know exactly how fast I
was going. I started out very slowly,

Over the next couple of months, I worked on getting into shape. I would
walk at first and then add in a little intermittent running. I discovered
"Couch to 5K" and downloaded the app to my phone. Little by little, I
got stronger. Finally, the day came when I was able to run a 5K on that
treadmill, very slowly, let me quickly add, but a 5K none the less. My
friend Arlene and I had started walking once a week also but running
was not in the mix. I continued to do all I knew to do.

Then one day I received a phone call from my friend, Kathy. She had
not been a runner either, but her church was starting a group to train
for a 5K. They would meet once a week, do a Bible study and do some

running. That sounded interesting. I knew I would not be able to attend the group meetings but then she asked the question.

"Would you train with me so we could run together in the fall?"

I was speechless. She knew I was blind and was quite aware of the responsibility involved in guiding a blind person, especially running. But she had no idea about my dream and effort to be a runner. I knew this was from God and the answer was, "Yes, I would love to!"

And we started doing some running outdoors. I discovered that running on a treadmill and running outdoors are two different things, but that did not deter me. We kept on running. We experimented with various ways for her to guide me and settled on a short rope that we both held on to. We learned how to navigate speed bumps.

Finally the time was getting close. I had continued to walk with my other friend but she did not know about my running endeavor. Kathy and I decided that she might like to do the 5K with us. I gave her the information and she was interested. I explained that she would need to get on line and sign up. That was all good. A couple days later, I got a call from her with an interesting question.

"Debby, I am on this website signing up for that 5K we are doing. They are asking if I am walking or running. We are walking, right?"

I was not sure how she had missed this but . . . "Actually, no. Kathy and I are running; you can walk if you like though."

There was silence on the line. Then she asked, "Running?"

"Yes," I answered. "Is that a problem? Again, you do not have to run."

Her response was immediate, "No, if you are running, I am running!" She told me later; she was not going to be outdone by a blind lady who was ten years her senior.

When we arrived at the park where the event was being held, Kathy pointed out that there were a lot of hills. We were not really prepared for that. Then I had an idea, "Let's run all the downs and walk the ups." We did. And we all ran; at 32°F I might add.

The three of us became great running buddies and participated in a number of runs over the next couple of years. It came to a halt when

Kathy fell, not on a run, and broke her leg in a couple of places. She needed to have surgery with a rod being placed in her leg. My other friend developed a serious lung condition, which made running impossible.

I was no longer running but I kept on doing some serious walking. At the beginning of 2020, I found out about a challenge that the parks and recreation department of my town was promoting, a 1000-mile challenge: to walk 1000 miles in a year. I did not find out about this challenge until around February 1 but I was interested and signed up. I did the math and realized that I would need to do 100 miles a month. That would give me some margin. I made sure my Fitbit was synced to my phone and I started clocking miles. Since it was in the middle of winter and cold outdoors, I mostly used a treadmill, sometimes at my house, sometimes at a local gym. All was going well until around the middle of March 2020. We all remember that big shut down for COVID 19. Of course, the gym closed. Then, for some reason, my treadmill stopped working. What was I going to do? I was not even sure that the challenge was going to continue. I tried to call the city office but of course, no one answered. They were shut down, too.

I had to make a decision. By this time, I was at around 150 miles. After consulting with my Senior Partner, I decided that I had come too far to quit now. I would keep going. I would continue even if the city did not. On a TV show, a doctor pointed out the importance of staying active, even and especially during the shutdown. He said to walk around your kitchen table if you have to. I rearranged some furniture and established a thirty-foot space where I could walk. I heard about a man from France who had been training for a marathon. It got canceled, but he decided that he would do one anyway. He had a seventeen-foot balcony in his high-rise apartment building and that is where he did his marathon! When the weather got warmer, I walked outdoors in my yard and in the neighborhood. I did not quit. The city did continue the challenge through 2020, 2021, and now in 2022, and I am all in! And, I am still doing the walking. My treadmill is working again, and I have a couple of walking buddies.

And what about the running, you ask? I say that I want to run a 5K with my grandson when he is twelve. He is eleven! I have not given up the thought of running again.

chapter seven

GRANDPARENTING—WHAT MY GRANDCHILDREN TAUGHT ME ABOUT GOD

When a friend from church had her first grandchild, she was ecstatic. I did not understand but all she said, with a big smile, was, "just you wait."

She was right! I thoroughly enjoy my grandsons. There is a big difference between children and grandchildren. Of course, I have actually never *seen* them, but we have a solid connection in spite of that. They understand my limitations and have adapted in terrific ways. They are fabulous with describing things to me and guiding me when I need help.

One day Carson spotted a bird's nest near the apartment. He immediately told me about it, describing it in great whispered detail: "So, there is uh, an adult robin sitting on the edge of the nest." We stopped walking so he could watch.

"Oh, and it has a worm in its mouth. And now there is a little baby bird with its mouth open." He was excited as he went on, "Oh, look, the mommy bird is feeding the baby with that worm."

I was so grateful for that description. "Carson, what we are seeing here is pretty special. Most people never get to see this. They see pictures of it but usually not in real life."

Then he had a question. "Gigi, have you ever seen this before?" He knew I had seen in the past.

I was honest. "No, Sweetheart. I have never seen this in real life."
With no hesitation he commented, "Well, *this* counts!"
I believe that I have a better understanding of God and His desire for relationship with us because of my grandchildren.

He Wants To Be With Us

While I was visiting Stephanie and the boys once in their tri-level home, Dane, age 7, called down to me from the family room above, "Gigi! Can you come and play with me?"
I had planned to help Stephanie with something but at that request, I told Stephanie I would catch her later and headed up the stairs to the family room.
"Sure," I said. "What do you want to play?"
His response surprised me. "I don't care. I just want to be with you."
And that is exactly what I think God is saying to us, "I just want to be with you."
On another occasion, Carson was heading to bed but he had a request, "Can we talk, Gigi?"
As a counselor, when someone asks if we can talk, I slip into counselor mode. And now, I was concerned. *What could possibly be so troubling to this young child?*
"Sure, Sweetheart. What would you like to talk about?" I settled in for a long conversation. Again, I was not expecting his answer.
"Oh, I don't care. You pick." He did not have a big troubling issue. He just wanted a connection with me.
Again, God feels that way towards us. He paid a big price to make that connection possible. We are often quite busy with a lot of things on our to-do lists. We seem to have difficulty working in time with Him, but He still says, "I just want to be with you."
He also sets boundaries for us.
At one point, the boys lived in a house that had a great driveway. There was enough room to ride their bikes and shoot baskets. Once when I

was with them, we were outside and they were playing in the drive and front yard.

"Just stay in the drive" I said as I stationed myself near the street end of the drive where I could hear exactly where they were.

"Don't go in the street," I cautioned the boys

"Why not?" Carson asked. It was an honest question.

"There are cars in the street and you might get hit."

There was a short silence and I imagined that he was looking up and down the street. "But there are no cars coming right now, Gigi."

In his mind, with his level of understanding, It seemed quite safe to play in the street but with a blind grandmother in charge, it was not happening. "I know, Honey, but there will be cars coming and I do not want to take a chance." Then I added for good measure. "If you cannot obey this rule, we will have to go inside."

He got it and we had a good time playing outside, in the driveway. Maybe he did not fully understand but he loved and respected me enough to follow my rules.

God has rules for us, too. We may not always understand completely but when we respect Him and honor His authority, we obey Him whether we understand it or not. It starts with the Ten Commandments in Exodus 20. Of course, if we choose to play in the street and do get hit by a car, we cannot really blame God.

He Shows Grace and Forgiveness

While this may come as a shock to some, our grandchildren are not perfect. There are times when they disobey us or are disrespectful. It is tempting to give them a pass but we know that this would not be good for them. God is like that with us as well. Being blind, it would have been easy for them to disobey me and do things of which they know I would disapprove. They might think they could get by with it. As good responsible grandparents, we cannot let that happen. We need to make the rules clear as well as the consequences. When they come to us with an apology and a repentant heart, forgiving them is easy. I realize that the purpose of this interaction, and our forgiveness, is restoring the relationship. We want that for our relationship with our grandchildren in the same way that God wants it for His relationship with each of us.

As I am writing this, I wanted to include a story of a time when my grandsons disobeyed me. It would be a time when I had to confront them and then forgive them as our relationship was restored. I am sure it happened. It had to have happened, I just said they are not perfect. But I cannot, for the life of me, remember a time like this. Maybe this is how it is for God who chooses to not remember our sins, who removes them as far as the east is from the west.

He Wants Us to Grow

During a time when one of the boys was learning to pronounce the letter *L*, it would sometimes come out sounding like a *W*. So he would make a firm statement, spoken with conviction, "I am wittle, but I am not a baby!" We love it when our children are small and helpless. We love caring for them but it would be tragic if they never grew. We want that for our grandchildren just like God wants that for us. We know what growth looks like for them. They get bigger. They are more independent. They make better decisions and become more trustworthy. They are less self-centered and begin thinking of others more. They learn things and are becoming more knowledgeable.

So exactly what does growth and maturity look like for us? The short answer, becoming more like Jesus.

Grandparenting Is a Mission Assignment

In my counseling practice, I have been amazed at the number of times a client would tell me that their primary spiritual growth has been from a grandparent. The conversation would go something like this:

"So, it seems that you have a good relationship with God?"

"Yes, I do."

"I guess your parents were Christians? Did they take you to church?

"Actually, no. My parents never went to church. It was my grandparents who came by and took me to church."

Sometimes parents are so busy with the other responsibilities of parenting that they overlook the importance of pouring spiritual truths into their children. It can be the grandparents who have a more relaxed and leisurely relationship with the children who make it possible to attend to this issue. It can take the form of reading Bible stories to the grandkids, helping them memorize Bible verses, or explaining spiritual truths. Sometimes it is playing a Bible-based game or going for a walk and talking about God in nature. Often it takes the form of simply listening and helping them process difficult situations with wisdom from the Word. I loved playing games with my grandsons. A favorite was a card game based on "Go Fish." The cards had pictures depicting the story of Jonah. I labelled the cards with Braille so I could play with them. I found a Bible *Monopoly* game which we played. While not in Braille, the boys assisted me with the visual parts of the game. The same was true for the game, *Pilgrim's Progress.* I made sure each of them had a Bible that they could understand and we enjoyed reading through Genesis together, me with my Braille version, they with their print ones.

The Bible has several references that point out the urgency of passing on spiritual truths:

> But the love of the Lord remains forever with those who fear Him. His salvation extends to the children's children. (Psalm 103:17 NLT)

> And this is my covenant with them, says the Lord. My Spirit will not leave them and neither will these words that I have given you. They will be on your lips and on the lips of your children's children forever! I, the Lord, have spoken. (Isaiah 59:21 NLT)

Of course, at the core of this mission is prayer. Many times these prayers are private but not always. It is vital that our grandchildren hear us pray. I was in the habit of praying for everything with my boys. It could be something like trying to find a lost object. It could be praying for healing of an injury. It was certainly my first suggestion when something seemed overwhelming. Once we were all together watching a ball game on TV. It was a really important game with our favorite team. The game was almost over and the score was really close. Carson and Dane were up pacing and talking to the players on the screen. All of a sudden, one of the boys came running over to where I was sitting on the sofa. "Gigi, we've got to pray!"

We did, and this time, the game went into overtime and our team won! At least, that is how I remembered it. But there is a bit more to this story. Shortly before publication, I reviewed this chapter with the boys. I told them the stories to get their confirmation. They understood and agreed with the various scenarios. They seemed to understand the underlying concepts except for the last one, the one about praying for the ball game. The conversation went something like this:

Carson: "Which game was that?"

Me: "I don't remember."

Dane: "I think it was the one between . . . " and he named two teams.

Carson: "Was I the one who asked for prayer?"

Dane: "No. It was me; I remember that."

Carson: "Was it the game around the holidays, maybe in December?"

Me: "Yes, I am pretty sure."

Carson: [after a thoughtful pause] "We did not win that game, Gigi. It was close and we did go into OT but we ended up losing. It was really close."

No one spoke for a moment.

I was tempted to just blow this off. After all, I thought I was finished with this chapter. Who would know anyway?

Oh, yes. My boys would know. They would know that I was alright with a little bit of untruth. And that was not okay!

Me: "So it looks like I will need to change how that chapter ends."
And so I did.
We continue to pray and God continues to be in charge!

chapter eight
SABBATH IS AN OBEDIENCE ISSUE

I n the previous chapter, I pointed out that God sets boundaries for us. There are rules we need to follow. These start with the Ten Commandments from Exodus. I thought I was doing pretty well with those, but one day I thought it would be good for me to read back through them, just to double-check. I did. I was a little caught off guard when I read verse 8, "Remember the Sabbath by keeping it holy" (Ex. 20:8 NLT, author's paraphrase).

That started a conversation with my Senior Partner, "So what exactly does that mean, Sir?"

This became another example of walking by faith, not by sight.

I remember having a conversation about this issue with a friend. He was reflecting on his day off.

"So was it a Sabbath?" I asked, thinking maybe I could gain some insight from his experience.

"Yes, it was a good day. I got a lot done."

"I do not think that is what the Sabbath is all about."

Over the period of several months, I decided that I would set aside one day each week and try to treat it as a Sabbath. It might not be Sunday since I usually am in ministry on that day. It might be difficult to make it a day of rest. It could be Saturday, but some weeks, that day was also not good. So, each week I would decide which day of a given week would work best.

Exactly what does one do, or not do, on a Sabbath? The two concepts that I understood about this day was that it would be a day of rest and that we were to keep it holy.

First, I learned that I had to pick the day and prepare, which included deciding what I would eat on that day and getting it ready in advance as much as possible. It meant informing those around me that I would not be available on that day and not scheduling appointments. That was not too hard.

The second part of establishing this Sabbath habit was actually quite difficult for me. I realized that I did not know how to have a day of rest. Yes, I had been on a lot of vacations. I had worked a fulltime job most of my life, so I understood having a day off each week. Usually those days were not days for rest, though. They were times to get caught up on other chores. I often would take a couple of hours to read, knit, or go for a walk. That was relaxing but I could not remember taking an entire day for rest and restoration. Probably the closest I came to that scenario was when I was sick on a rare occasion and had to go to bed to rest. I did not think that God was talking about this. So, yes, having a day for rest was a new concept. I struggled with feeling guilty. I decided I would give it a shot, make myself do nothing for a day, nothing that fell into the category of work for me. That meant not setting my alarm for a wake-up time. Yes, I would have my devotional time as usual. Then the rest of the day would be filled with things that were relaxing for me.

Keep It Holy

Then I remembered that the text of Exodus 20:8 actually says "Remember to observe the Sabbath day by keeping it holy." What exactly does that mean? How does one make a day holy? Perhaps it should include things that would enhance my relationship with God. Perhaps my goal should be to draw closer to God throughout that day. It might include conversations with Christian friends. Perhaps it would include journaling or reading a good book. Maybe it would mean going for a long walk and having a conversation with my Senior Partner.

The first couple of times I attempted to observe a Sabbath, I was pretty uncomfortable. I felt guilty just doing nothing but resting. Our culture tells us that we should be productive at all times. We often can justify taking a couple of hours off or even half a day, but a full day seems excessive. I kept working on it, though. It soon began to feel good. If I thought of something that I needed to do, I would write it down so I could do it the next day. By the end of the day, feeling more relaxed and refreshed, I realized how badly I needed this time.

God knew we would need this once a week, and that is what Jesus meant when He said, "The Sabbath was made to meet the needs of people and not people to meet the requirements of the Sabbath" (Mark 2:27 NLT).

The first observation of the Sabbath likely was when the children of Israel were in the wilderness with manna to eat. They found the manna each morning, enough for that day. On the sixth day, though, there was enough for two days so they did not gather food on the seventh day. The Sabbath was a gift to them (Ex. 16:29).

Over the years, it seems that many of the Jewish leadership got it wrong. They turned the Sabbath into a day governed by a complicated set of rules and regulations, which was far from the day of holy rest God intended the Sabbath to be.

I still do not get my Sabbath habit right every time but I am closer than I have ever been in the past. I am going to keep working on it, obeying, and walking by faith.

chapter nine
THIS WRITING JOURNEY

W hen in my twenties, I had the opportunity to write my story, *Debby* by Deborah Zook. I mostly focused on the process of losing my sight and how I adjusted, relying on God at every turn. Since that time, I have done some more writing, some even for publication. I've done some devotionals for our church's *God's Word for Today* as well as some journaling. My desire for more writing has never gone away; actually, it has gotten stronger over the years and now, in March 2022, it is time!

As I talked with my Senior Partner about this, the details gradually came into focus. These included the title and a tentative outline for the book. I wrote the first chapter, "The Water Slide." Since it involved my grandsons, I wanted them to read it and make any corrections in case I got some of the details wrong. They did, and I made the necessary changes. But then one of them had some questions.

"So, Gigi, when will you have this book done?"

I had not really thought about that but I knew I needed to come up with an answer.

"In about six months."

But then there was another question.

"How many chapters will it have?"

I did not know that either but since he wanted an answer, I came up with one.

"Probably around twenty," I guessed.

He was satisfied but now the pressure was on.

And I jumped into chapter two.

This would be an interesting journey. It seems I have been traveling down this path for some time, perhaps most of my life. It would be exciting to share how God has walked with me through difficult and challenging times. At this point, I was not sure what all this would entail but I was all in. It certainly felt like a moment when I was most walking by faith, not by sight.

On the morning of March 28, I made a Facebook post from Psalm 18: "You light a lamp for me. The Lord, my God, lights up my darkness. In your strength I can crush and army; with my God I can scale any wall. (Ps. 18:28-29, NLT).

As I thought about it, I questioned what this verse would look like if I was writing it. Yes, armies and walls apparently were issues for David but not so much for me, though I did have issues. Written as I understood it, the verse would likely read something like this, "You turn my uncertainty into clarity with clear direction. With Your help, I can complete this book in six months, covering the areas You indicate. With Your help I will have the courage to be transparent, for Your glory."

And I was off and running!

After completing a couple more chapters, I shared some of these thoughts with a friend. She was encouraging and asked some questions. As I explained where I thought God was leading me, she said, "I will want to get some copies. It sounds like this is exactly what my sister needs to read. She knows you and I think she would enjoy this. I will need to get one for my father also. Actually, I can think of several others who would benefit from this."

If the book had been available in that moment, she would have walked away with a couple of copies. I knew I could not quit!

I imagined that my Senior Partner was sitting across the room listening. I think I heard Him clear His throat. He was making sure I did not miss the significance of this conversation. I didn't and I kept on writing.

After eight chapters were done, I had gone through the list of topics that I thought He had given me. There would be some editing, but for the most part, I thought I was done. I decided to go for a walk and as I walked, I asked Him, "So, am I done?"

I was surprised when I felt He said, "No."

I did not say anything at first but I was thinking, *Really?*

I asked for some clarity, "But, didn't I cover each of the areas You put on my list? Didn't I talk about each of them?"

"Yes, you did. You were walking by faith, not by sight. I had given you those thoughts, those areas to cover and you did as I asked. Yes?"

"Yes, that's right," I answered, still puzzled.

"Now I want to give you some insights that you had not thought of sharing before. These are truths from my Word as they have played out in your life experiences. They are areas that I need my people to think about. Are you good with that? I realize you do not know exactly what I am talking about right now but I will reveal it all to you as you start to write. This will continue to be walking by faith, not by sight. Okay?"

"Yes," that was okay.

Immediately, I remembered a conversation I had recently and I knew that was where He wanted me to go next.

"But would that be the last chapter?" I asked. I thought I needed to know. He said, "We'll see." And I felt Him smile.

Then He added, "In the past, you have written as you had time, squeezing it in often after everything else was done. I need that to change. I want this writing to go to the top of your priority list. I want you to write first, then squeeze the other things in. Can you make that change?"

I thought about it. He was right, of course. Yes, I could make that change. Would that mean I'd have to take some things off my plate?

I recalled a time in the past when I was quite busy. Everything I was doing had significance and was good. I took this issue to Him saying, "I am just too busy. I have way too much on my plate."

I expected Him to feel sorry for me or tell me to just work harder and stop complaining. To my surprise, He agreed with me.

"Yes, you do. But some of those things are things that I did not put there." He gave that some time to sink in and then He added, "And if you would like, I can help you figure all that out. You need to fulfill your commitments but when that commitment is complete, do not accept anything new without asking Me first."

That is exactly what I did and over the next couple of months, things lightened up. I became more focused on what He had for me to do. Perhaps I had allowed my plate to get too full again. Perhaps it was time to reassess my priorities. Perhaps a re-evaluation of my time commitments would be an essential part of this writing journey.

chapter ten
WHO AM I?

Recently, I participated in a 5K fundraiser. Of course, being blind, I had assistance, a kind lady who was willing to run or walk with me. We each held the end of a short thick rope. She let me set the pace and I actually did some intermittent running. On the back of her shirt, she had a sign that read, "GUIDE." People coming from behind us would be alerted that I was blind. In addition, as we would approach a group of people ahead of us, she would call out, "Blind runner on your left." Everyone was very kind to make room for us. All went well and though I beat my previous time, it was nothing special.

The interesting thing was this. It had been years since I had a guide like this for running. In the past, I resented anyone pointing out my blindness, drawing attention to me in that way. I always wanted to be seen as fully sighted, no limitations, no special need for assistance. I realized that this time, I felt different. I had no such thoughts and was not at all uncomfortable with this action which was keeping us all safe. So, what had changed?

Accepting My Blindness

As I gradually lost my sight, I had a hard time accepting this loss with its accompanying limitations. As a child, I only knew one person who was blind. He was a kind and loving gentleman who attended our church. In addition to blindness, he had a cognitive delay and a serious speech impairment. Perhaps I pushed back on my sight loss so hard because I associated being blind with those other disabilities. During those college years when I was losing my sight, I tried hard to not let anyone know I was having trouble with my vision. Even after I started using a cane, I tried to be as independent as possible, even refusing assistance in situations when it would have been easier and safer for me to accept help. I did not think I was in denial. After all, I was using a cane and reading Braille. But I was not realistic regarding my expectations for myself. I did things that most blind people would not do. I climbed ladders to put Christmas lights up on the front of my house. I drove a friend's truck in the parking lot of the church when He asked me to help pull out shrubs. God kept me safe and provided friends to help, even at times when I did not realize that I needed the help.

I am not sure what triggered the change but a couple of years ago, things started to shift. I began to accept the reality that I was limited by my blindness and that made me different from people around me. Again, something pretty obvious to everyone but me. I connected with other blind and visually impaired people through the American Council of the Blind and their affiliates. I've developed a great deal of respect for the accomplishments of many of these individuals.

The result of this new acceptance of myself was quite surprising. For some reason, I thought I needed to prove something. Perhaps it was pride, trying to be someone, something, that God did not intend for me to be. Being honest about this was quite refreshing and liberating. I stopped pushing back on who He created me to be, blindness and all. Yes, there are some things we can change about ourselves sometimes. I can lose some weight and I am working on that, but I cannot change the fact that I am blind. He knows that about me, He actually planned it that way and He has a reason.

Trusting Him in this area was another big step in the growth in our relationship. How can He possibly work this for good? But He has and He continues to do so.

So, does Ephesians 2:10 really apply to me? Am I really His masterpiece? Did He really create me in His image to do good works? Did He really prepare all this in advance?

Yes! Yes! And yes!

Embracing Our Identity

Discovering, accepting, and embracing who God created us to be is a big deal. It is a game changer. We often get information about our identity from an early age. Parents and other adults in our lives tell us who they think we are. Sometimes they get it right but often they don't. As we grow into adulthood, we carry that picture of ourselves with us. We need to come to grips with that image of ourselves that was painted for us back then. Then it is up to us to determine if it is correct or not. Sometimes our faults and shortcomings are the primary thing we focus on in our lives. God sees who we are in this moment but He also sees who He created us to be.

While in the midst of writing this chapter, I had an opportunity to process these ideas with my grandson, Carson, age eleven at the time. He listened carefully, asking questions from time to time for clarification. As I explained my first contact with a blind person, he got it. He pointed out, "So everyone has a purpose no matter how different from normal we think it is."

Pretty good insight for eleven years old.

This is where hearing from God is essential. He says that we are a masterpiece. He says He calls us sons, no longer servants. He says He has plans for us to prosper. What great news! But do we really believe this?

And now we are back to walking by faith, not by sight. We may not feel that we are a masterpiece or a child of God. We may not think we look like someone who is prospering. People around us may not treat us like we have great value. He says it, though, and that makes it true. We simply need to believe Him and live it out.

chapter eleven
DID SOMEONE MENTION LOSING WEIGHT? WHY IS THIS SO HARD?

Most people I know would like to drop a few pounds. Many have health issues directly or indirectly related to being overweight. When I started this book, writing about weight loss was not on my list. I could identify several areas and times in my life when I walked by faith and not by sight but losing weight was not in the mix. He, my Senior Partner, indicated that I should include this here. I am doing that, walking by faith, but I'm not at all certain where this will go.

Thinking about Psalm 18:27, I realized it applies to losing weight, "You rescue the humble, but you humiliate the proud." Again, walls and armies were issues for the Psalmist but not so much for me. I do have challenges, though, and getting to an ideal weight is certainly one of them. So, I could rewrite the verse to say, "With God's help I can write this book. With His help, I can lose the weight I need to lose."

Like most of us, I have lost and gained a lot of weight throughout my life. The number of eating and weight loss plans available to us is overwhelming. How does one even start to get a handle on what works, and even more importantly, what will work for me. I have redefined my relationship with food and it seems to be working for me. I think I am supposed to share some of the principles here.

The Why

Assessing our motivation for most things we do is crucial to our being successful if we want to change our habits. I believe my Senior Partner wanted me to be clear about this for myself. You might want to think about it too.

Here are several reasons why we might want to lose weight.

One: Wanting praise from people. This actually was my motivation at one point in my life. Even though I was blind, I knew that being over-weight was not attractive. I wanted my friends to think well of me. But, of course, this is a terrible motivation. You may or may not get the affirmation you think you deserve.

Another motivation for being at a good weight is so we can be healthy and live a long life. It does not take much of a deep dive to understand the relationship between extra weight and overall health. The problems range from diabetes and heart problems to joint issues and energy levels. These are great reasons to want to be at a healthy weight. For me, though, that long range goal was not compelling enough to influence my food decisions on a day to day basis.

A third reason seems somewhat noble, to be a model for others. I might want to be at a healthy weight so my friends will benefit from my example. They might see what I am doing on this journey and be proud of me but that is no guarantee that this will result in them doing the same thing. I would be setting myself up to be disappointed.

After doing some soul-searching, I asked Him what really made the difference this time. I have wanted to lose weight for decades, but there were a couple of things that contributed to me being willing to make some changes. First, I noticed a decline in my energy level. I was feeling sluggish and getting drowsy at times. Yes, I am in my early seventies but I was not alright with this change. I wanted to continue being my best in ministry and in my relationships, including with my grandchildren. Somehow, I knew my being overweight was a factor in this. I wanted to be fully available to please my Senior Partner and be the best version of myself that I could possibly be. I know that He loves me and has a great plan for my life. He created me and knows exactly what it will take for me to be happy and fulfilled. I do not want to miss out on anything He might have in store for me, especially if it is something I might miss because of bad food choices.

Around that same time, Stephanie shared with me a change she had made in her eating pattern. It was a plan, a philosophy, that focused on eating real food coupled with a simple tracking system. I listened and did some reading on my own. It made sense. I gave it a shot. And it is working. I have lost twenty-two pounds at the time of this writing. I still have a bit more to go and am leaning on my Senior Partner to know just when I have lost enough.

Food Is Fuel

Our cars, lawn mowers, trucks, and planes all require fuel. That fuel varies from one vehicle to another. They are not interchangeable. In addition, there are different quality levels within each kind of fuel. A poor quality fuel will result in the machine not performing at its maximum potential. If we think of food as fuel for our bodies, we easily can understand that what we put into our mouths makes a difference in how our bodies function

This is not how we usually think of food though. Most of us who are overweight will readily admit that we like to eat. We can name our favorite restaurants and exactly what we would order off each menu. Recently, some friends and I were going out for breakfast. When they picked me up, the decision as to where we would eat had not been made. I had narrowed it down to the three main ones they likely would choose. In addition, I had even decided exactly what I would order at each one. Yes, I like to eat.

On another occasion, I was with my friend, Joy, and we were going to a coffee shop. It was relatively new and she had never been there so I was giving her a little information about what I thought was good.

"So have you been here before, Debby?" She asked.

"Yes," I answered. "A few times."

As we stepped up to the counter, the waitress greeted us warmly and then added, "So, Debby, do you want your usual?"

What could I say. Busted!

Back to the "Food is fuel" idea: God has generously provided us with a wide variety of food unlike that manna that the children of Israel had in the wilderness. We can then be strong and healthy to do His work. Often, though, we turn it into something more. Sometimes I like to eat to reward myself. Perhaps I have had a tough day and I think I deserve a reward. Food often does the trick. I might feel sad or down and think that something sweet will lift my spirits. But when we eat for other reasons than for fuel, we give food power over us, which gets us into trouble. There is nothing wrong with rewarding ourselves or having a way to lift our mood. Using food for this, though, is dangerous. We need to find a better way to do that. And the options are endless.

I brought this up with my Senior Partner. I came to understand that I relied on food to meet some basic emotional needs. It was hurting me, though. I needed to move in a different direction. Just thinking about not having some of those comfort foods readily available, though, made me a bit sad. I actually felt disappointed when I considered that I needed to find something besides food to meet these needs. I like eating. Have I mentioned that? But I realized that this was not working for me. I trusted Him enough to realize He had a better plan.

F-A-K-E Sources of Fulfillment

There are a couple of other areas we can mistakenly depend on for fulfillment.

Food—This is probably at the top of the list for most people. We need food to survive physically, but when it becomes a source of happiness and fulfillment, we likely will get into trouble.

Approval—This is out of balance when we need approval from the significant others in our life to feel fulfilled. Sometimes, we'll do things that we know are not the best for us but we are so desperate for approval that we do them anyway. Then there might be times when we are more concerned about what those around us think than what would please God.

Knowledge—I like to learn new things. There is fulfillment in this for me but it is not lasting. There is always something more to learn and explore. If this is what I rely on for fulfillment, I will always be frustrated. Also, a desperate desire to learn new things can consume a lot of time.

Entertainment—This can include a lot of things—TV, movies, ball games, eating out, playing games. All of these things are good but when they get out of balance, when we become dependent on them to be fulfilled, we are in trouble. We can come to need to be entertained to be happy.

These are all fake sources of fulfillment and they will not provide lasting contentment and fulfillment.

So, what are some of those things that provide lasting fulfillment? Here is my list. (Some of yours may be different. It would benefit you to think about it and make your own list.)

- Quality time with my Senior Partner.

- Reading His Word.

- Connecting with a positive friend.

- Going for a long walk.

- Reading a good book.

- Working on a hobby, creating something.

- Listening to or creating music.

So I changed my relationship with food and my eating patterns. Once I made this shift, using food for fuel and only fuel, things started to change for me. Yes, I still like to eat but eating is now in its proper place, serving me, making me strong and healthy.

Qualities of a Good Eating Plan. Some Food for Thought…

As I have thought about all the different eating plans available to us, the ones I have tried and the ones I have just heard about, I was able to create my own plan, one that works for me. Here is a list that I created of qualities that seem important. See what you think.

Sustainable for My Entire life

The problem with "going on a diet" is that, one day, you will go "off" that diet. That is when many of us put all the weight back on, and more. I needed an eating plan that I could live with the rest of my life. It would need to be a plan that was satisfying and healthy but would not leave me feeling deprived or hungry. I needed a plan, not a diet!

Affordable

Some plans cost money. Sometimes they might be worth it. This is especially true when we think about the money we save on medication and doctors visits. But how long can we continue putting out this money? And, when the money runs out, will we feel like we have to go back to our old eating habits?

Close to Nature

Again, God has given us a wide variety of food options, unlike that wilderness manna. We have done an amazing job of turning a lot of that food into something that is not healthy for us. Potatoes get turned into French fries. Wheat becomes donuts. Bananas are often served as banana splits. Cherries get loaded with sugar and are served as pies. A good goal would be to eat food as close to nature as possible.

Good Hydration

Most of us do not drink the amount of water that is recommended. Not all liquids serve to hydrate us. Some have the opposite effect. Our bodies and our brains need water to function at maximum levels. Feeling thirsty is our bodies telling us that we need water. Sometimes we may actually think that we are hungry when we really are thirsty.

Pursue God

I can hear what you are thinking: "So are you really going to try to spiritualize this whole food and weight issue?"
Yes, I absolutely am. Hear me out.
I believe that there are times when the hunger we sense, while quite legitimate, is not really a hunger for physical food. It is a desire for more of God. It could come from not feeling loved and appreciated. It could be that we feel like a failure and that we are not living up to expectations. We could feel lonely. Each of these scenarios, and others, have a spiritual root. Each of them can be minimized or completely resolved through a deeper, closer relationship with God. As that relationship grows, that hunger diminishes as it is fulfilled by that closeness to God. He invites us to come close to Him.

"Give your burdens to the Lord and He will take care of you. He will not permit the godly to slip and fall" (Ps. 55:22 NLT).

And if that were not enough . . .
We are created for connection. Sometimes we have healthy blood families and that is wonderful. That is not always the case, though. His church is a family that provides the relationships we long for. In a healthy church family, we find connections that provide ways to give and receive love. We are able to help others, giving us a sense of purpose. We have opportunities to learn and grow in a lot of areas.

chapter twelve
"JUST SIT DOWN!"

F or several years, I spent nearly half my time in Tennessee to be near my family. It was about a two hour drive and, of course, I had to find rides. God, amazingly, made that possible. Sometimes I could get a ride with someone for the entire trip. Usually, though, someone would take me part way and another person would meet us there and give me a ride for the rest of the way. On one of these occasions, the schedules did not match perfectly and I was going to need to wait at the midway point for my connection. I decided to wait at a small coffee shop. They had little tables outside where I would be able to sit and work on this book.

Stephanie and I went inside and got our drinks. She helped me get to a good table. I had my luggage, my computer bag, and my purse. We both had drinks and I was using my cane. I was not sure how this would all work out so as she led me to a table, I asked, "What can I do to help?" I am not sure how she did it but she had managed to get everything in place. With a smile, she said, "Just sit down."

We hugged and she asked again if I would be alright. I assured her that I had enough to do to keep me busy for a couple of hours. She was satisfied and she turned and headed to her car.

And I sat down!

That statement sounded familiar to me. Where had I heard it before? Not in those exact words, but several times over my life, my Senior Partner had said this to me. It was usually at times when I had overloaded my schedule and felt overwhelmed. In those times, I would have too much on my plate and would feel frazzled.

I remembered a moment when one of my grandsons demonstrated this feeling in an interesting way. As a toddler, he had just discovered the fun sensation of going round and round in circles. The goal was to get so dizzy that he would fall down, giggling.

I found him in the middle of one of these moments one day.

"What are you doing, Sweetheart?" I asked.

He did not slow down but simply answered. "I'm trying to get busy!"

Of course he meant *dizzy*. While this is a fun activity for a toddler, it is not as productive for an adult who needs to get some things done. Sometimes it does feel like we are just getting dizzy, though.

On the exact day that I wrote this story, an interesting message showed up in my inbox. It was in response to the Bible reading assigned for that day, "Be still and know that I am God" (Ps. 46:10).

"I'm restless. My to-do list, not only the projects need my attention, but the people, too.

"The clock is ticking. Everything is urgent. My wife can confirm that I don't do 'still' very well. I prefer to be busy. Activity is my default reaction. My mind spins. The gears turn, sometimes grind. The list is reduced and things get done. But my heart is in turmoil.

"My emotions are frayed. It's difficult to rest and my sleep is fractured. I know there is so much to be done. My solution to my stress is found in the spiritual discipline of stillness.

"And yes, it does feel like punishment. While I don't do waiting very well, I've NEVER regretted stilling the 'never-done' list and taking time to quiet my mind and wait on God. Best still, acknowledging God's sovereignty over me is required to quiet my anxious thoughts and ease the tension of things undone. In the quiet, I hear God say, 'Rest now, I'm in control.'"

I immediately wrote back, "Just sit down!"

Isaiah 26 makes a great promise: "You will keep him in perfect peace, whose mind is stayed on you, because he trusts in You" (Isa. 26:3 NKJV).

The challenge is keeping our focus "stayed" on Him.
Isaiah 40 says it well:

> He gives power to the weak,
> And to those who have no might He increases strength
> Even the youths shall faint and be weary,
> And the young men shall utterly fall,
> But those who wait on the Lord
> Shall renew their strength;
> They shall mount up with wings like eagles,
> They shall run and not be weary,
> They shall walk and not faint.
> (Isaiah 40:29–31 NKJV)

The key here is waiting; not the easy thing to do, but well worth it.

Worth the Wait

> God is not on our schedule,
> Sometimes we think He is late;
> But His plan is good,
> His Word is true,
> And it will be worth the wait!

chapter thirteen
FOURTH QUARTER

I need to talk about this aging thing. You may not be there yet but some day you will be and likely someone you know and love is already there. It is an interesting process with a lot of pitfalls and possibilities. God's Word addresses it: "Therefore we will not lose heart because even though we are growing older, our spirits are being renewed day by day" (II Cor. 4:16).

And here's my take on it.

Fourth Quarter

When some people reach a certain age
It seems their life is done;
Yes, they still do have birthdays;
But they don't seem to be having fun.

So I have made a decision,
I will not be that way.
Each year is a gift from God
And I will celebrate the day.

Yes, I've had a wonderful life,
Many joys along the road;
Some might say it's time to coast,

Let others carry the load.

But the ball game isn't over
After one quarter or two or three,
It is what happens in that fourth quarter
That tells what the score will be.

So as I celebrate this birthday
I know exactly what I'll do,
I'll give this fourth quarter all I've got.
I'm only seventy-two!

A few years ago, an older couple moved into our area and started attending the church. They were delightful and we loved having them with us. Apparently, they had been active in churches in the past and seemed frustrated that they were not playing a major role in the life of the church.

"I am not doing anything," she would comment.

I tried to assure her that at eighty-nine and ninety-one, it was just great having them walk in and participate in the worship service. "Just having you guys here is wonderful. Seeing those smiles and hearing those kind words is a blessing to us all."

I am not sure she believed me but I meant it.

Another friend, Marion, had a similar concern. "I don't seem to have anything to do," She commented one day. She was no longer able to get out much and could not come to church. I thought for a moment and then suggested, "Have you ever thought about sending little notes of encouragement to people? Marion hesitated and then admitted that she thought God had been telling her to do just that. I offered to provide any materials she might need, cards, stamps, addresses. She assured me she had everything she needed. I knew that a note of encouragement from this senior saint would lift anyone's spirit.

She had been a friend for years and knew my daughter when she was small. When I visited, she would always ask about her. I would be sure to keep her informed about what was going on in Stephanie's life. When my grandsons came to town, I made certain that we visited her. I wanted Marion to stay informed about Stephanie and the boys but I had another more important motive. Marion was a prayer warrior. I knew that once she met the boys, she would pray for them. I valued those prayers!

Marion had another gift that she shared with us. She liked to memorize poems. When she ran across a poem that ministered to her, she would take the time to put it to memory. And some of them were quite long! Then, when we'd visit her, she would recite them for us. I never grew tired of hearing them. Toward the end of her life here on earth, Marion lived in a nursing home. She soon made friends and was a blessing to those around her. Since I knew how much she loved poetry, I decided to write a poem for her. It would not be a poem that would just be read at her funeral. I would read it to her myself. And I did! In addition, I had it printed and framed. She kept it on the dresser in her room, a tribute to how much of a blessing she had been to so many.

Here it is.

Marion

I have this really special friend; Her name is Marion Tharpe.
She has some trouble getting around But her mind is really sharp.

She loves to recite her favorite poems and she knows quite a few;
And if you ask her nicely, she might say one for you.

She has spent a lifetime spreading God's marvelous love,
In so many wonderful ways, she is a gift from above.

I think I know the reason why she is still here today;
Because more than anything else, Marion loves to pray.

She prays for everyone she knows; she names them
one by one.
And only eternity will reveal all the victories those
prayers have won.

But she says she's ready to go to receive her reward
in heaven.
I don't know what's the rush, . . . She's only ninety-seven!

I thought you'd like to read a couple of those poems Marion memorized. Here are my two favorites:

Jonah

Now listen, my children, I'll tell you a tale,
How old Jonah, the prophet, got caught by the whale.

The whale caught poor Jonah and bless your dear soul,
He not only caught him, but swallowed him whole.

A part of this story is awfully sad,
It is how a big city went to the bad.

When the Lord saw those people with such wicked ways,
He said, "I can't stand them more'n forty more days."

He spoke to old Jonah and said, "Go and cry

To those hard-hearted people and tell them that I

"Give them forty days more to get humbled down
And if they don't do it, I'll tear up their town."

Jonah heard the Lord speaking and he said, "No,
That's against my religion and I won't go!

"Those Nineveh people mean nothing to me,
And I am against foreign missions you see."

He went down to Joppa and there in great haste,
He boarded a ship for a different place.

The Lord looked down on that ship and said He,
"Old Jonah is fixing to run off from Me."

He set the winds blowing with squeaks and with squeals,
And the sea got rowdy and kicked up its heels.

Old Jonah confessed it was all for his sin;
The crew threw him out and the whale took him in.

The whale said, "Old fellow, don't you forget
I am sent here to take you in out of the wet.

"You will get punished aright for your sin."
So he opened his mouth, and poor Jonah went in.

On beds of green seaweed that fish tried to rest,
"I will sleep while my food I digest."

He got mighty restless and sorely afraid

And he rumbled inside as the old prophet prayed.

The third day that fish rose up from his bed
With his stomach tore up and a pain in his head.

He said, "I must get to the air mighty quick,
For this filthy backslider is making me sick."

He winked his big eyes and wiggled his tail
And pulled for the shore to deliver his male.

He stopped near the shore and looked all around,
And vomited old Jonah right up on the ground.

Old Jonah thanked God for His mercy and grace
And turning around to the whale, made a face.

He said, "After three days I guess you have found
A praying man, old fellow, is hard to keep down."

He stretched himself out with a yawn and a sigh
And sat down in the sun for his clothing to dry.

He thought how much better his preaching would be,
Since from Whale Seminary he had a degree.

When he had rested and dried in the sun
He started for Nineveh most on the run.

He thanked his dear Father in heaven above
For His tender mercy and wonderful love.

And though he was nearly three days late,

He preached from the time he entered the gate.

Till the whole population repented and prayed
And the great Hand of justice and vengeance was stayed.

Children, when tempted to disobey, remember this tale,
And if you run from God's call, look out for the whale.

And should you stay away from the sea,
God may send an elephant after thee.
—Anonymous

But my favorite one is The Kite.

The Kite

Once upon a time a paper kite
Was mounted to a wonderous height
Where, giddy with its elevation, it thus express'd
self-admiration.

"See how yon crowds of gazing people
Admire my flight above the steeple;

How would they wonder if they knew
All that a kite like me can do!

Were I but free, I'd take a flight
And pierce the clouds beyond their sight.

But, ah, like a poor pris'ner bound
My string confines me near the ground.

I'd brave the eagle's tow'ring wing
Might I but fly without a string."

It tugg'd and pull'd while thus it spoke
To break the string, at last it broke.

Depriv'd at once of all its stay,
In vain it try'd to soar away.

Unable its own weight to bear,
It flutter'd downward through the air.

Unable its own course to guide,
The winds soon plung'd it in the tide.

Ah, foolish kite, thou hadst no wing,
How couldst thou fly without a string!

My heart reply'd, "O Lord, I see

How much this kite resembles me!
Forgetful that by Thee I stand, Impatient of Thy
ruling Hand.
How oft I've wished to break the lines Thy wisdom for
my lot assigns?

How oft indulg'd a vain desire for something more, or
something high'r?

And but for grace and love divine, a fall thus dreadful
had been mine.
—By John Newton

So, yes, our bodies will age and we may struggle with health issues along the way. But our spirits can be renewed day by day. We can always continue to grow. That is pretty exciting.

chapter fourteen
GROWING AS WE WALK BY FAITH

Several years ago, I had a vision; I think that is what you would call it. It was a mental picture that was quite vivid and meaningful to me and still, to this day, I think about it. In this image, I am walking down a path. It seemed to be a dirt path, not one that was particularly difficult but not very wide. I was following someone who I understood to be Jesus. He was not too far ahead of me and I knew I was to keep my eyes on Him and stay close. I was also aware that He was keeping close tabs on me there behind Him.

I seemed to be doing fine with one little exception. On each side of this path, from time to time, there were people standing along the edge. They seemed to be friendly types. I had no sense of fear or danger. They were, however, reaching to me, wanting to take hold of my hand. It was clear that they wanted me to come with them, off the path. Although it was quite tempting, I knew that if I went with any of them, I could not follow where Jesus was leading me.

Reflecting on that image all these years later, I understand that this has been my greatest temptation throughout my life: not staying in my lane. I like exploring new things, trying things I have never experienced before, learning new concepts. The problem, though, is that I can easily get out of my lane, go down a path not intended for me, which ends in disappointment and I miss out on what God has planned for me.

Growing Is Part of God's Plan

Growing and changing are parts of life and they happen all around us in nature. A giant tree starts as a small seed. Looking at that seed, one would never guess its potential. It looks nothing like the tree it will one day become. And think about the changes that take place inside the womb as that sperm and egg unite. As that embryo grows and develops, it takes several different forms. Finally, that little baby emerges but that is certainly not the end. That child grows and changes over years. And what about that caterpillar? Growth involves major changes for that little guy, too. The butterfly that emerges looks quite different from the furry little worm it started out to be.

God intends for us to grow spiritually, as well. We start out pretty wobbly but as we spend time with Him, we get stronger and more focused. There are several ways to frame this growth issue.

Asking, Seeking, Knocking

Matthew 7:7 gives us an amazing promise, "Ask and you will receive, seek and you will find, knock and the door will be opened" (Matt. 7:7 NKJV).

I used to think that asking, seeking, and knocking were simply different ways of saying the same thing. But there are some subtle differences that are significant in terms of our spiritual growth. Asking is the starting point. It means that we have a connection with that person and we are making our needs known. We are clear about where we are and what we need. Seeking, hunting, searching adds a level of action on our part; now we are not just having a conversation, we are up actively going after what we want. Often, there are some things we can do to bring about the spiritual growth we desire.

Knocking adds another whole element. It gives us a picture of a door, likely closed, that we would like to have opened. It implies that when that door opens, we plan to step through. It suggests that we are willing to make changes, to live in a new place. It is our request for admission. Yes, He wants us to ask. He wants us to go deeper and seek. And yes, He wants us to knock and then be willing to step into His will for us.

The Obedience Perspective

At first, we obey what God is telling us to do because we are afraid not to. We know from the Word that there are negative consequences for disobedience. As we grow, we choose to obey because we have come to understand that there are blessings that come from obedience. The problem with both of these motives, avoiding trouble and gaining blessings, is they still have our focus on us and our needs. Growing spiritually takes us to a place where we obey because we love Him and want to please Him. It no longer is about us and our comfort. It is about Him and pleasing Him. Then, we come to realize that we are on mission for Him. It is not just about avoiding negative consequences or gaining blessings. It now has even gone beyond pleasing Him. Now it is about seeing the world, the people around us, our jobs, everything, as part of a bigger picture. We buy into His big picture of bringing salvation to the world. Obedience simply is doing what He asks us to do to further the kingdom whether we understand it or not. We know that He has chosen us and it is a privilege to serve Him in whatever way He chooses. We are part of His team. It truly is not about us!

Priorities

Another way to think about growth is in terms of our priorities. When we are young, it is all about us and our comfort. One of a child's first words is, "mine." As we mature, we begin thinking about those around us and what is best for them. We understand that God is our source and He will provide everything we need. We slip away from accumulating things and trying to gain approval from others. We know that if we are pleasing to our Lord, nothing else matters.

Jesus sets the bar as He taught and modeled servanthood. He washed feet, touched lepers, and fed the hungry. He told the disciples that typically people want to lord it over others, to see themselves as powerful. We tend to want people to do what we say, to meet our needs and build up our egos.

And then He adds, "Not so with you" (Matt. 20:26).

The more our focus is on pleasing Him and looking to Him to get our needs met, the more effective we will be in life and ministry.

Often in my counseling office, I ask, "So was there a time in your life that you would say that you were closer to God than you are right now?" Most often, the answer is a regretful, "Yes."

"Was that a good time in your life?" I press.

The answer is always the same. "Yes, absolutely."

"And would you like to go back there?" I already know the answer, of course they would.

The next question is not as obvious. "Do you know how to do that, to get back to that place? I was not sure, at first that they would understand how this happens. But after a little reflection, they always do. And now they have an action plan. I encourage them to get back to where they left off in their closeness to God but then to think about getting even closer. Over the years my conversation has changed as I interact with Him first thing each morning. At first, I simply made my plans with no thought about Him. My priority has shifted, though. I came to where I would present my plans to Him and asked Him to bless my efforts. That felt pretty spiritual. At least now, I am letting Him know what I want. Then, as I grew, the question shifted to, "So, what do you have for me today?" I had come to understand that usually my plans fell far short of what He had on my agenda. I came to understand and accept that if my day turned out differently than I had projected, it was alright. My to-do list might not be the same as His. I might not get to check off very many items on my list but as I followed His lead, I would have accomplished what was on *His* list for me. This is far more important.

Then there was another shift. The question became, "How can I serve You today?" This changes everything. The people who come across my path are no longer interruptions to a carefully planned agenda, they are divine appointments that are far more important than what I had planned. At the end of the day, I can ask, "So, how did I do, Sir? And yes, I am available tomorrow, also. How can I serve you?"

And life gets better and better. We never fully arrive. There is always another level of experiencing God, a deeper abiding, a fuller sense of His love. I tell Him I want to get closer than I have ever been before. I have even said that I want to be closer than I have ever known anyone to be. I do not know exactly what that means but I believe that is His plan for me . . . for each of us!

One more thing!

Another way of seeing this relationship is portrayed in a poem I found one day. It is framed and hanging in my home. Here it is.

The Touch of The Master's Hand

'Twas battered and scarred, and the auctioneer
Thought it scarcely worth his while
To waste much time on the old violin,
But he held it up with a smile.

"What am I bidden, good folks," he cried,
"Who will start bidding for me?
A dollar, a dollar" then, "Two!" "Only two?
Two dollars, and who'll make it three?

"Three dollars, once; three dollars, twice;

Going for three . . . " But no,
From the room, far back, a gray-haired man
Came forward and picked up the bow;

Then, wiping the dust from the old violin,
And tightening the loose strings,
He played a melody pure and sweet
As sweet as a caroling angel sings.

The music ceased, and the auctioneer,
With a voice that was quiet and low,
Said, "What am I bidden for the old violin?"
And he held it up with the bow.

"A thousand dollars, and who'll make it two?
Two thousand! And who'll make it three?
Three thousand, once; three thousand, twice;
And going, and gone!" said he.

The people cheered, but some of them cried,
"We do not quite understand
What changed its worth?" Swift came the reply:
"The touch of the master's hand."

And many a man with life out of tune,
And battered and scattered with sin,
Is auctioned cheap to the thoughtless crowd,
Much like the old violin.

A "mess of pottage," a glass of wine;
A game—and he travels on.
He's "going" once, and "going" twice,
He's "going" and "almost gone."

But the Master comes, and the foolish crowd
Never can quite understand
The worth of a soul, and the change that's wrought
By the touch of the Master's hand.

—By Myra Brooks Welch